Introduction:

Crested Geckos were once thought to be extinct, but since their rediscovery in 1994, they have quickly become one of the most popular pet reptiles in the trade. The ease of care and gentle disposition of Crested Geckos (*Correlophus ciliatus*, formerly known as *Rhacodactylus ciliatus*) is a large reason that they have become so popular for both beginner and expert reptile keepers alike. There is no doubt that Crested Geckos will remain one of the most popular pets worldwide, for a long time to come.

The Crested Gecko gets its name from the fringed projections that run from above the eyes, resembling eyelashes, down their back to their tail. They are sometimes referred to by other common names such as, New Caledonian Crested Gecko, Guichenot's Giant Gecko or Eyelash Gecko. They are also referred to as just "Cresties".

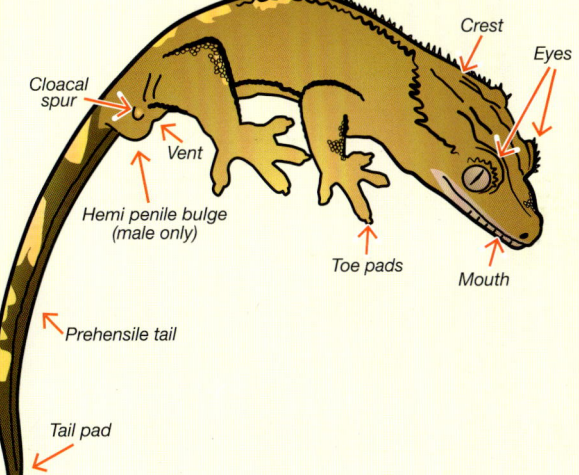

Crested Geckos are typically 7-8 inches (17.5-20 centimeters) in total length with a snout to vent (STV) of 3.5-5 inches (8.5-12.5 centimeters). Crested Geckos can be a very long lived pet. They will generally live 7-10 years, but have been kept for 15 years or more.

Natural History:

The Crested Gecko is native to a cluster of islands northeast of Australia called New Caledonia. This is a habitat of tropical forest with moderate, year round temperatures. Crested Geckos are nocturnal which means they are active at night. They are arboreal, spending most of their time in the lower levels of the forest canopy in search of the fruits, nectars, and insects that make up their diet.

Crested Geckos have many unique characteristics. They do not have eye lids, so they have developed the ability to lick their eyes to clean them. They also have specially adapted toe pads that allow them to climb very smooth surfaces. Crested Geckos are among the few lizards that have a prehensile tail which allows them to wrap their tail around branches, like a monkey.

Fun Fact: The gecko's toe pads and the tip of the semi-prehensile tail are covered in small hair like structures called setae that hold on to most surfaces, including glass.

Caging:

Crested Geckos are arboreal, which means they are most comfortable in cages that are taller, to allow space for climbing. Zoo Med's Naturalistic Terrariums® are a great choice for housing Crested Geckos. The NT-2 (12" X 12" X 18" tall) is a great size enclosure for 1-2 adult Crested Geckos. If you want to house more than two adults it may be a good idea to upgrade to the larger NT-4 terrarium (18"X 18" X 24" tall). In most homes, the relative humidity is quite low compared to the natural habitat of your Crested Gecko. Using a glass Zoo Med Naturalistic Terrarium® will help maintain higher humidity. The ReptiBreeze® screen cage can be used to house Crested Geckos, but will require more attention from the owner to maintain the environmental needs of these geckos. It is recommended to use a glass Zoo Med's Naturalistic Terrarium® until you are exceptionally familiar with the requirements of keeping Crested Geckos.

Naturalistic Terrarium NT-2

Heating and Lighting:

Keeping Crested Geckos at the proper temperature is important for maintaining good health. Ideal temperatures for Crested Geckos are 72°-78°F during the day. A nighttime temperature drop down to 65°F is tolerable. This is generally room temperature in most households. If additional heating is required, a low wattage Moonlite® or Nightlight Red™ bulb can be used. Crested Geckos do not thrive if temperatures are too hot and should never be kept above 85°F. Remember to always use a thermometer like the Zoo

ReptiSun® 5.0 UVB

Nightlight Red™

Moonlite®

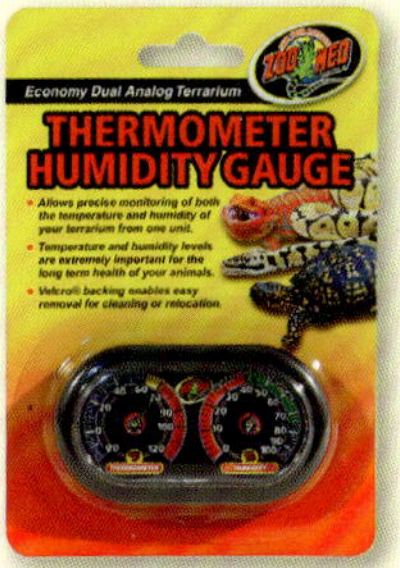

Med Dual Thermometer Humidity Gauge to accurately ensure proper temperature.

A UVB light source, such as a ReptiSun® 5.0, may be a good addition to the cage. Although Crested Geckos do not require UVB lighting, recent research has shown that they will benefit from exposure to low levels of UVB lighting.

Thermometer Humidity Gauge

Humidity and Water:

Humidity is an important part of a Crested Geckos environment and should be maintained around 60-80%RH. This can be achieved by misting daily and using a substrate such as Eco Earth®, which holds in moisture. Crested Geckos drink water droplets from the glass and are nocturnal, so it is a good idea to mist the cage each evening just before geckos become active. Be sure to use ReptiSafe® to remove any chemicals from tap water before misting the cage. A ReptiRain® can be used to automatically mist the cage for a low maintenance set-up. Use a hygrometer to confirm proper humidity.

ReptiSafe®

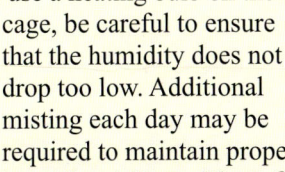
ReptiFogger™

Keeping the cage and decorations clean is important because Crested Geckos will drink water droplets off the glass and decorations. To do this, routinely disinfect the cage & decorations using Wipe Out 1™. In addition always keep a dish with clean water available for the geckos to drink.

If you need to use a heating bulb on the cage, be careful to ensure that the humidity does not drop too low. Additional misting each day may be required to maintain proper humidity. A HygroTherm® can be used in combination with a ReptiFogger® for automated heat and humidity control. If your cage becomes excessively wet, let the cage dry to prevent mold and bacteria growth.

ReptiRain®

Wipe Out 1®

Substrate:

Eco Earth® coconut fiber is a highly recommended substrate which will help maintain proper humidity. At a depth of 2-3 inches, this substrate will also allow females to demonstrate natural nesting behaviors. Repti Cage Carpet™ and Eco Carpet™ can also be used as an easy to clean, reusable substrate. Additionally, Zoo Med's New Zealand Sphagnum Moss™ or Frog Moss™ can be added to the cage. This moss can be layered on top of the Eco Earth® or Cage Carpet™ to add a pleasant, natural look to the terrarium while maintaining humidity.

Eco Earth®

Decorations:

Arboreal species like Crested Geckos benefit from having plants to climb on. Zoo Med's Natural Bush Plants™ make great cage decorations that allow for climbing behavior. The plastic leaves can be cleaned easily and when the cage is misted, collect water drops for your gecko to drink.

Natural Bush Plant™

It is important to provide a place for the geckos to hide. Zoo Med's Repti Shelter™ and Turtle Hut™ both make great options for hiding. Other excellent decorations include Cork Rounds and Cork Flats. These natural cork bark hides allow a place for geckos to sleep during the day and climb on at night. Twisty Vines and Naturalistic Flora® can be added to give a natural look to the cage. The Repti Hammock™ gives geckos a ledge to hang out on and adds extra surface area to the cage for climbing. Some animals will choose to sleep on a Repti Hammock™ as well.

Naturalistic Flora®

Live Plants as Decorations:

For a more natural enclosure you may want to set up your Crested Gecko's cage with live plants. This can be done, but may require a little extra effort. You will need a light source to keep the plants alive that will not overheat the cage. For smaller cages, using an Zoo Med Ultra Sun® Compact Florescent Bulb will be sufficient to grow the low light tropical plants that are recommended for Crested Geckos. Given that Crested Geckos are heavy bodied, they require sturdy plants that will not break under their weight. Do not use toxic plants and be sure to wash the plants well so you are not introducing fertilizers or pesticides into the gecko's cage. Here are some plants that are a good choice for a Crested Gecko habitat:

- Pothos Vines
- Philodendrons
- Ficus Tree
- Sansevieria (Known As: Snake Plant or Mother-in-law's Tongue)

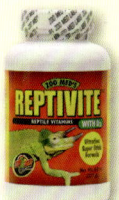
Reptivite™ with D3

Feeding:

Feeding Crested Geckos is an undemanding task. Zoo Med's Crested Gecko Foods™ meet the unique dietary needs of these animals. Research reveals that these geckos and their relatives eat a variety of foods including insects, small vertebrates, fruits, flower parts, pollen, nectar and even tree sap. This powdered meal replacement may be fed as dry power or mixed with water. Follow the feeding instructions on the package for best results. Crested Geckos should be offered a new dish of this powdered diet every day for juveniles and every other day for adults.

Repti Calcium® with D3

Crested Gecko Food-Juvenile

Crested Gecko Food-Adult

Handling:

Crested geckos are great pets that tolerate being handled and are very fascinating to interact with. Juvenile Crested Geckos are naturally a little jumpy. This is a natural defense tactic. They generally won't bite, but will try to jump to safety. To get your geckos acclimated to handling, it is best to start holding young animals for up to 15 minutes a day until they are sub-adults. Given that they jump periodically, it is best to hold them while you are low to the ground so that the gecko can't hurt itself if it falls. Avoid pulling a Crested Gecko from its cage because its prehensile tail may be wrapped around an object and this may cause it to drop its tail. Try and coax it to walk onto your hand. If a Crested Gecko drops its tail, it is best to put it back in its cage to reduce stress. It will heal up rather quickly, but unlike many other lizards and geckos; Crested Geckos can not regenerate their tails. The gecko will still live a happy life without a tail, but it is best to avoid this trauma if possible. After handling any animal, be sure to wash your hands.

Repti Shelter™

Compatibility:

Male Crested Geckos are territorial and should not be housed together. If kept together males will typically fight and cause injuries to each other or worse. Multiple females in one cage, or a male and several females can be housed together comfortably. Observe your geckos on a regular basis. If an individual is losing weight or has lost its appetite, it is best to isolate that animal from others. Set up another Naturalistic Terrarium® until that animal is back to good health. It is rare for Crested Geckos to fight, but occasionally they will mistake each other's tails as a prey item. This frequently happens when juveniles are kept in crowded conditions.

Crested Gecko female

Crested Gecko male

Breeding:

Crested Geckos are a fun, undemanding, and interesting reptile species to breed in captivity. They do not require noticeable seasonal changes to be replicated in order to breed. Clutch sizes of two eggs makes for a manageable breeding project. This two egg clutch size is seen in most gecko species and will prevent a beginner breeder from being overrun with hatchling geckos too quickly; however, Crested Geckos can produce ten to twenty clutches per year.

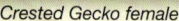
New Zealand Sphagnum Moss

If you choose to keep a male and female together, they will almost certainly breed. The male will usually bite the female's neck during courtship, but this should not harm the female. It is recommended to prevent male geckos from breeding with a female until the female is a minimum of one year in age and in good health. Breeding too early can stunt future growth of the female.

Crested Gecko hatching

Zoo Med's Guide to Crested Geckos   6   ©Zoo Med Laboratories Inc., 2014

Once the female is gravid and ready to lay eggs, she will dig in the substrate looking for a moist secure area for her nest. If you set up your terrarium with a 2-3 inch layer of Eco Earth®, the female will usually dig down almost to the very bottom of the terrarium and lay two oval-shaped, white eggs. They usually lay their eggs along a structure in the cage. If you are using any other type of substrate you will need to set up an egg laying site. The best way to accomplish this is to add a medium Repti Shelter™ and fill it 2/3 full of Eco Earth® and/or New Zealand Sphagnum Moss. Any egg laying area must be kept moist (but not wet) at all times. Rarely will you see the female nesting as she will be secretive and will usually do so during the night. It is a good idea to check the cage frequently when you are expecting eggs.

Incubation:

After the female gecko has laid eggs, proper incubation is exceptionally important in order to successfully hatch your baby Crested Geckos. Start by carefully removing the substrate to find the eggs. Once you have located the eggs, remove them being conscientious not to rotate the eggs. Reptile eggs should not be turned the same way bird eggs are. The recommended temperature for incubating eggs is between 72°-80°F. This can be achieved

Reptibater® Digital Egg Incubator

by using a ReptiBator® reptile egg incubator. Follow the incubator's instructions and have this set up in anticipation of the eggs. Now, set up the eggs in an incubation container. Use a small plastic container or deli cup with a lid and punch a few small holes to allow for air circulation within the container. Put these holes near the top of the container so the incubation material does not block the holes. Vermiculite is a commonly used media to incubate eggs. This can be acquired from a specialty reptile shop or at a garden center. If you purchase it from a garden center, be sure that it does not have any fertilizers, pesticides or herbicides. Put a small amount of vermiculite into the incubation container about one inch deep. Add water to the vermiculite at a ratio of 1:1 vermiculite to water by weight. Use your finger to make small indentations for each egg, then set the egg down without rotating it and cover the egg approximately half way with some of the moist vermiculite. Now add a lid to the container and place it in the incubator. The eggs will usually hatch in 65-120 days depending on the temperature. If you see the vermiculite starting to dry out you can add small amounts of water taking care not spray directly on the eggs. There are many different types of media and techniques used to incubate Crested Gecko eggs, but the factors are all the same. Keep humidity high and the temperature somewhat consistent. If eggs start to mold, they may not have been fertile or the incubation substrate may have been too wet. Continue checking the eggs, without disturbing them, while you wait for the baby Crested Geckos to hatch. Commonly the eggs will sweat beads of water just before the baby cuts its way out of the egg.

Hatchling Gecko Care:

The care of hatchling Crested Geckos is typically the same as caring for adults. They can be kept in smaller cages like a small Naturalistic Terrarium® (12"x12"x12") but keep in mind that smaller cages tend to dry out faster. Low humidity can be hard for juvenile Crested Geckos to handle. Spray the cage 2-3 times per day to keep the humidity over 70%. It is especially important to offer appropriate sized feeder insects to juvenile Crested Geckos.

Juvenile Crested Gecko

Color Patterns / Morphs:

With many Crested Gecko breeders working on selective breeding, there are many color and pattern varieties appearing in the captive Crested Gecko population. These color and pattern varieties are commonly referred to as morphs. Here are some of the commonly obtainable morphs as of this books printing:

Background Color:

The standard body color of a Crested Gecko can change substantially, so sometimes you will hear people talking about their "fired up" patterns. A "fired up" Crested Gecko is usually seen in the evenings, at night, or when breeding, when the gecko is at its most vibrant color.

- Light Brown – This is your "normal" morph - tan skin sometimes a little grey.
- Chocolate – Deep browns, almost black at times.
- Red – These geckos usually have a daytime tan color but at night will show a vibrant red color.
- Lunar – White background color which rarely darkens.

Body Markings:
- Pinstripe – This morph has two solid white stripes all the way to the base of the tail.
- Patternless – One solid color with little or no pattern.
- Bicolor – Similar to the patternless, but with a different solid color on the back of the gecko.
- Black & Tan – Also known as the "Oreo" morph because the pattern is

dark against very light.
- Dalmatian – A morph with black and white spots, and sometimes red, covering its body.
- Ink Blotch – Similar to a Dalmatian but many of the spots will be large like an ink blotch; not always fully round.
- Fire – A morph with a lighter head and back, as well as between the front and back legs. These areas are patterned like flames coming up the sides.
- Harlequin – Similar to the Fire morph, with the pattern also on the front legs.
- Stripe – This morph has a solid lateral white stripe between the dorsal and ventral areas.
- Tiger – Streaks of color, resembling tiger stripes running down the length of the gecko.
- Brindle – Similar to the Tiger but with more stripes that sometimes spread to the limbs as well as the body.

Crested Gecko Dalmatian

Crested Gecko Harlequin

Health:

Crested Geckos are a naturally hardy gecko species, but occasionally, they could have some health concerns. Most health issues can be avoided with proper husbandry. Here are some things to look out for.

Repti Shedding Aid™

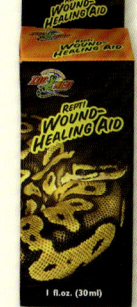
Repti Wound Healing Aid™

Improper Shedding and Dehydration:

This is usually an issue if the cage humidity is too low. A Crested Gecko is most vulnerable to low humidity and dehydration when shedding. Crested Geckos eat their shed skin to recycle the nutrients. Especially with young geckos, dry skin may get stuck. This is referred to as a "dry shed". If this happens, immediately separate this gecko from any cage mates. Increase the humidity and offer a Repti Shelter™ with moist New Zealand Sphagnum Moss. This gives the gecko shelter and someplace to rub to help start the shedding process. Keep a very high humidity of 80-90% until the shedding process has been completed. Zoo Med's Repti Shedding Aid™ can help with this problem by moistening the skin. By keeping up on the proper humidity/misting, this health risk can easily be avoided.

Dropped Tail:
Crested Geckos can drop their tails but it is a natural defense to avoid predators in the wild. Unlike other geckos, Crested Geckos do not regenerate a new tail. It is not uncommon to see adult crested geckos without tails. If your gecko loses its tail, the most important thing is to be sure that the cage is clean, to prevent the gecko from getting an infection. Repti Wound Healing Aid™ can be applied to the wound to prevent infection and help the wound heal faster. It will heal very quickly and your gecko will be fine. If the wound ever appears to be a green or yellow color, it may be infected and the animal should be seen by a reputable exotic pet veterinarian.

Floppy Tail Syndrome:
When a gecko has floppy tail syndrome, its tail will bend away from the body at an unnatural angle. There is some debate between breeders as to what causes this. This is when a gecko chooses to rest out in the open with its head down and tail in the air behind it on a glass wall, its pelvis will sometimes weaken to allow the tail to look floppy. Once a gecko has this syndrome it usually will not heal into a normal position. To avoid this, keep many cage decorations and hide locations available for the gecko to exercise. Keep calcium levels up in the diet, and avoiding dehydration may also help prevent this.

Metabolic Bone Disease (MBD):
With a proper diet and good supplements this will not be an issue. If a gecko has improper calcium and vitamins in its diet, it can develop weak bones. This can be avoided by Feeding Zoo Med's vitamin rich Crested Gecko Diet. Female Crested Geckos that have produced a lot of eggs and have depleted their calcium reserves are the most at risk. Additional Repti Calcium with Vit/D3 can be mixed into their diet and dusted on feeder insects to increase the calcium intake. If the gecko has Metabolic Bone Disease it is best to take it to a exotic pet veterinarian for treatment. A list of veterinarians can be found at www.arav.org.

Internal Parasites:
Crested Geckos are generally captive bred and therefore will not normally have problems with internal parasites. If your gecko stops eating, is abnormally skinny, and/or has unusually strong smelling, runny feces, it may have internal parasites. It is best to take it to a veterinarian to have a fecal exam done. A veterinarian will most likely need a fresh fecal sample from your gecko to determine if your gecko has any internal parasites and to decide on the best course of treatment. Crested Geckos are very good at hiding the signs of parasites until they get stressed. To avoid getting your pets sick, always quarantine any new gecko before putting them in with your other animals already in your collection. Always wash your hands and use a hand sanitizer between and after handling other reptiles.

Summary:

Crested Geckos are becoming one of the most well-liked, first pet reptile choices. A Crested Gecko is a good choice for most people because they are not a challenging pet and are naturally docile. Almost every Crested Gecko offered for sale is captive bred, as a result will be accustomed to captive conditions and do not have the issues associated with other species of wild caught reptiles. If you want a fun and educational reptile to add to your home, a Crested Gecko is an excellent choice for you.

Other Geckos of Interest:

Here are some other types of geckos that reptile keepers enjoy that have similar care and requirements to Crested Geckos. Do not mix species in the same terrarium. If you are going to acquire any of the following geckos, each species will need its own cage.

Gargoyle Gecko

Gargoyle Gecko (Rhacodactylus auriculatus)

This gecko is similar to a Crested Gecko in care. They have a stockier build and don't use their prehensile tail as often as a Crested Gecko. Gargoyle's have slightly higher protein demands than Crested Geckos, so feeding insects twice per week is preferred. These geckos will also eat Zoo Med's Crested Gecko Diet. They can regenerate their tail. Similar to Crested Geckos, Gargoyle Geckos are also native to New Caledonia.

Mossy Gecko or Prehensile Tailed Geckos (Mniarogekko chahoua)

The availability of this gecko species in captivity is starting to increase. They are larger than Crested Geckos. They have a slightly higher protein demand than Crested Geckos, thus feeding insects twice per week is preferred. These geckos will also benefit from Zoo Med's Crested Gecko Food™. There are two main localities that are offered: Mainland & Pine Island, New Caledonia.

Mossy Gecko

New Caledonian Chameleon Geckos (Eurydactylodes agricolae & Eurydactylodes vieillardi)

These small Chameleon Geckos have a very unique look to them and have a similar care to Crested Geckos. They do not get as large as Crested Geckos with most adults only reaching six inches. They eat Zoo Med's Crested Gecko Food™ as well as small insects.

Mourning Geckos (Lepidodactylus lugubris)

Mourning Geckos do not make good pets to handle, but they do make a very attractive gecko to keep. This active little gecko is full grown at just over four inches in length. This gecko will make a very hushed chirping noise in the early evening. This small "house gecko" is also parthenogenic which means they are all females and they lay fertile eggs that they glue to the cage or decorations. The babies are identical to their mother. They can be raised on a diet of only Zoo Med's Crested Gecko Food™ but they can also live on an insect only diet.

Day Gecko

White-line Geckos or Skunk Geckos (Gekko vittatus)

This is a gecko found throughout Southeast Asia. They are a large, thin gecko that eats more insects than Crested Geckos, but will also eat Zoo Med's Crested Gecko Food™. They like a higher humidity and temperature than the other species listed so far. Once acclimated to captivity White-lined Geckos will breed regularly.

Day Geckos (genus Phelsuma)

There are many species of Day Geckos. The main difference with keeping Day Geckos as opposed to Crested Geckos is that they are active during the day, as the name suggests. Being a diurnal species, these geckos will require a small Repti Basking Spot Lamp™ along with a Repti Sun® 5.0 UVB bulb. This UVB lighting is very important for Day Geckos to thrive. Many Day geckos may rip off their skin when trapped. This means that it is very important not to restrain these geckos so handling them is not recommended.

Electric Blue Gecko (Lygodactylus williamsi)

Male Electric Blue Geckos have the most vibrant blue coloration of any reptile, while the females are olive green in color. They have the same care re-

Electric Blue Gecko